CONDO BUYING

MISTAKES

46 COSTLY MISTAKES
CONDOMINIUM BUYERS MAKE

...AND HOW TO STEER CLEAR OF THEM

MATT LEIGHTON

Copyright and Disclaimer

Table of Contents

Introduction 5

Section 1. Before You View the Condo 7

Section 2. Viewing the Condo 13

Section 3. Writing Your Offer and Going Under
          Contract (Opening Escrow) 28

Section 4. Living in the Condo 41

Share the Knowledge 44

Referrals 45

Contact Information 46

Introduction

The goal of this book is to highlight the most common mistakes buyers make when purchasing a condominium. Whether you are a first-time home buyer or a seasoned investor, use this book as a resource when purchasing your next condo to ensure that you are not making a costly mistake.

I have worked with hundreds of buyers and sellers in the Northern Virginia condo market and see people making at least a few of these mistakes on a weekly, if not, daily basis.

Before we get started: If you are not already following me on social media, you can find me on Instagram, Facebook, YouTube and Twitter where my handle is @TheMattLeighton. I would love to connect with you!

This book is broken down into the four general sections of the condo-buying process. I encourage you to skip around to the section that interests you the most and revisit the different sections as you go through the condo-buying process.

Without further ado, let's begin.

Section 1. Before You View the Condo

1. Not Understanding Rental Restrictions

Rental restrictions in condo associations usually break down into two categories. The first is the length of which you are allowed to rent out your condo. Most associations will only allow leases that are six months or longer in duration. If you are thinking about buying into a condo community for the sole purpose of using it as an Airbnb or short-term rental, think again.

The second way in which rental restrictions can affect new condo owners is that some communities have a waiting list for owners who are looking to turn their primary residence into a rental property. I know of at least one condo in my market that has a rule that states once the community is 45% renter-occupied, every additional owner that wants to rent out their unit has to put their name on a waiting list.

Rental restrictions can be cumbersome depending on the association, so you may want to call the management office or have your agent call the office before you submit your offer to make sure that any future rental plans are within the rules and regulations of the community.

2. Not Knowing the Pet Restrictions

If you already have a pet, chances are you have previously lived in a community where you had to get prior approval before moving in, so maybe you have already done your due diligence when looking at pet-friendly communities. However, if you are thinking about getting a pet, or maybe your significant other is planning on moving in with their pet, you want to be sure to verify the pet rules and restrictions.

Restrictions can vary significantly by community. The least restrictive example I have seen is one condominium that allows an unlimited number of pets. But what some do not realize is that restrictions often come down to breed and even weight restrictions. I have even heard one story of a condo board forcing an owner to put their dog on a scale to verify it was under 45 pounds. That poor puppy!

3. Ruling Out a Community Because of a High Condo Fee

When working with buyers that have specific purchasing criteria, we will often place a cap on the monthly condo fee. While seemingly harmless at first glance, this might severely limit the client's purchasing options.

Condos with higher condo fees may have a much lower sales price. These condos may include all utilities. And they may even have larger floor plans that you didn't think were possible at your price point.

Of course, it should be noted that higher condo fees also are associated with condos at both ends of the pricing spectrum. Uber-luxury condos will have astronomical condo fees, while condos that are seemingly from the Mesozoic era will also run you a high monthly rate.

But simply ruling out an entire group of potential condos because of the monthly fee may be handicapping your search.

Price without value is meaningless. A $500 monthly condo fee for a one-bedroom may seem high, but if it includes all utilities, 24-7 front desk concierge, a parking spot, and an outdoor pool, are you sure you want to rule that condo out of contention?

While it may not be your first choice, communities with higher condo fees than normal should be given a chance because they offer a "wildcard"-type inventory that may not have been on your radar before.

4. Over-Emphasizing Online Review Sites

I am not sure what it is about apartments and condos, but for some reason the only time that people review large multi-family buildings is when a (former) resident has a complaint. Seriously, look up a large complex in your area on a third-party review site and see what the reviews say. I can almost guarantee you that a majority of the reviews will be negative.

While it's important to research a building's reputation, try not to internalize online reviews. While looking at reviews for the building I live in, I noticed that a few of the reviewers didn't even live in the building! One reviewer was visiting a friend and another reviewer was a contractor. Both reviewers left one-star reviews.

How can you review a residential community without even living or having lived in the building?

Online reviews usually represent the extremes. The building is probably not as bad as the negative reviews make it out to seem. But there could be some truths to the drawbacks mentioned online. And the community is probably not as heavenly as the good reviews make it out to be. Take online review sites with a grain of salt.

5. Waiting Until the Spring to Buy

Conventional wisdom says that the best time to buy a property will be in the spring time, when there is the most inventory available. That being said, there is a surge of properties that become available after Labor Day and some units will hit the market in the winter time.

If you are looking for condos in the "off-season", you will usually have less competition and a better chance at scoring a discount.

The "best" properties may become available in the spring, but those condos will also attract the most amount of interest and will result in the winning buyer over-paying.

An alternative would be to consider looking at properties available in the fall and winter, buying at a lower price, and then using the difference in price to add your upgrades in the fashion that you want to make the property your own.

The spring market comes and goes quickly. You can find condos for sale in every month of the year.

6. Not Checking Whether the Building is Approved for FHA or VA Financing

One of my first clients I ever had was using an FHA loan to purchase his condo. When we finally submitted the offer, I was excited at the possibility of finally closing my first sale.

That excitement was short-lived as the listing agent emailed back almost immediately and said the community was not FHA-approved and they could not even consider the offer.

If you will be purchasing your condo with an FHA loan or a VA loan, you and your agent will have to research whether or not the condominium communities are approved for this type of loan. The best way to do this is to simply fire up your web browser and search "FHA-approved condos" or "VA-approved condos." One of the first results will be a site that you can enter in your specific city that will then provide you with whether or not the specific development is approved.

And if you were wondering, the likely reason that condo communities are not FHA-approved is that the ratio of renters-to-owners is too high. When there are more investor-owned properties than owner-occupied homes in a development, the likelihood that people will default on their loan is higher.

7. Not Researching New Development Projects for Nearby or Adjoining Lots

If you are purchasing a condo near or next to a vacant lot, a surface parking lot, or a property containing multiple dilapidated buildings (i.e. old strip mall), be sure to research land records to get a better understanding of the future of that parcel.

Your property value will be affected by neighboring lots. Things like construction right outside your window, a new building that blocks your view, or even a new development that you do not agree with like a stadium, gun store, or affordable housing complex could be your new neighbor.

8. Buying at Your Max Budget Instead of What You Actually Need

Your lender will want to spend as much as possible. Your real estate agent will want you to spend as much as possible. Your friends who have never bought a condo before will tell you that you're making the right decision buying a massive and high-priced condo.

Take a step back and think about what you really need. It may make sense for you to buy a two-bedroom condo if you are by yourself. It may make sense for you to buy a three-bedroom condo if it's you and your significant other.

There should be a reason for you to be buying at the top of your budget other than the fact that you can afford it.

Will you be renting out the other room? Turning it into a home office? Do you have a baby on the way?

It is okay to slowly grow into a condo that's too large for you now. Game plan before your search on how long you will be living in your condo and how much space you will require, now, and in the future.

Section 2. Viewing the Condo

9. Living Next to the Loading Dock

When viewing condos, have an understanding of the exterior surroundings of the building to get an idea of noise or disruptions that may occur outside your unit or within the vicinity. The location of the loading dock should be a priority, especially if you work from home or enjoy sleeping in on the weekend. The constant idling of delivery trucks or the flow of moving trucks in and out of the loading dock garage may be a nuisance to units within earshot.

Move-ins can be loud and disruptive, but the main reason we want to know the location of the loading dock is for trash pick-up. Even opening up your window a crack will increase any noise into your unit tremendously. Imagine thousands of bottles and trash crashing down from the dumpster into the trash truck every day, every other day, or weekly. Depending on your noise threshold and your daily schedule, living next to the loading dock (or the neighboring buildings' loading dock) could be a significant disruption in your life.

10. Not Viewing the Parking Spot

It amazes me how many people rely on their car every single day, but when it comes to viewing a condo to purchase, the parking spot becomes an afterthought. I met with a landlord the other day who told me that her tenant called her in tears once because she was having difficulty parking her large SUV in the garage parking spot.

In some markets in my area, parking spots sell for up to $50,000 and sometimes even $100,000 in downtown D.C. Even if you do not have a car or do not drive that often, the parking spot can be a large asset when it comes to resale value that you can rent to another resident in the meantime. You want to ensure that there is nothing wrong with the spot and that the spot can fit a normal to large car if you own a vehicle or if you are planning on renting out your spot.

11. Buying Near a Fire Station or Major Highway

Location is everything but there are some city infrastructure components that you should be weary of. Buying near a fire station, a major highway, or another loud neighbor could pose a problem not only for your sanity, but also when you look to resell.

In my market of Arlington, VA, those fire stations located near condominium communities say they wait a few blocks before turning on their sirens. Fair, but there will inevitably be the firefighter that will get trigger happy and turn on the siren too early. If you are living near a fire station, it is not a matter of "if", but it is a matter of "when."

When you're touring a condo and you look out your window to see the highway below or off in the distance, try opening a window or going out on the balcony. How's the noise? Go to the master bedroom and stand very close to the window and just listen. Your agent might look at you funny. But there's nothing funny about traffic, cars honking, engines revving, sirens blaring, and other highway noise when you are trying to get your beauty sleep.

12. Not Checking the Direction the Unit Faces

Natural light is important, and it can also be deceiving. I have worked with buyers that enter a unit with their cardinal direction app on their phone, and if it is not facing the correct direction, we walk back out in a matter of seconds.

While this may sound a little ridiculous, there is some reasoning behind the practice. Those buyers are looking for southern exposure that would bring the most amount of light into their residence. If you are viewing a condo with northern exposure in the summertime in the afternoon, it may appear that the unit receives excellent natural light. But imagine the condo in the peak of winter, when the days are shorter and sunlight is harder to come by; your northern-exposed condo will be struggling to receive natural light.

One trick to see the natural light is to turn off all the lights when you are viewing the property (assuming you are seeing it during the daylight). I know when I am the listing agent on a property that does not receive a lot of natural light, I will sneak over to the property before another agent shows the unit to turn on all the lights to prove how bright the unit is. Counter this by turning them all back off again!

13. Not Checking Whether Extra Storage Is Included or Available

In one-bedroom condos, and even two-bedroom condos, closet space is a top priority. Storage is at a premium, and every coat closet and shelf is necessary. So why is it that buyers often for-go checking to see if an extra storage locker included?

In some communities, extra storage can be valued as much as $10,000. Yet when coming up with comparable properties and valuing one condo versus another, buyers often omit this information. Extra storage is critical for both coming up with comparable sales figures and, well, coming up with extra storage.

Every community is different. Some condos come with storage. Others may not. In some you can even rent storage units from the management company. And are you out of luck if your condo does not come with a storage unit? Maybe not... I know one condo owner in my area that buys other people's storage units and rents them out. He's up to five and looking for more!

14. Not Checking the Age of the HVAC and Water Heater

The good news about living in a condo is that most of your expenses will be taken care of and you are only responsible for what is inside your walls. The bad news is, that still leaves the opportunity for costly repairs, mostly when it comes to your HVAC unit (furnace and A/C) and your water heater.

When you do your home inspection, pay close attention to what your home inspector has to say about the major utility systems. The age of the units will be important, but the condition will be just as valuable. A one-year-old HVAC system that has significant signs of wear-and-tear could be a worse situation than a ten-year-old system that is spotless.

Most HVAC systems have a lifespan of 10-20 years. But even if you have an older system, that does not necessarily mean it will fail imminently. Condos are usually on the smaller end and, since you will be heating and cooling 1,000 square feet or so, systems can last a long time.

If you are moving into a condo that has an old HVAC system or a rusty water heater, start making a contingency plan for when either (or both) fail. You can also negotiate repairs or replacement into your home inspection contingency. Note: Perfectly "good"-looking units can fail at any time. It's better to start saving for a new system now, than be surprised and shocked when the system does fail.

15. Falling in Love With a Condo That's Staged

Staging works. It makes spaces feel bigger, it can brighten up rooms, hide imperfections, and help to give purchasers an idea of how to furnish oddly shaped areas. There is nothing wrong with buying a staged condo per-se. Where you will end up making a mistake is *overpaying* for a condo that is staged because you put too much emphasis on the decorations.

Staged condos look and feel significantly better than vacant units. Condos with no furniture can feel cold and unwelcoming, whereas condos that have been professionally staged seem inviting and friendly.

Staging can play tricks on your eyes. (Side note: staging consultants are geniuses and you should use them when you sell. They can make your entire condo seem like it belongs in a magazine). Often, a full bed will be used in the master bedroom, or a smaller sofa will be put in the living room to show off how large the space is. Alternatively, large, over-sized furniture could be used to also show off how large the space is. The exact pieces of furniture and style will be chosen by the seller and the stagers.

Take a step back and ask yourself if your furniture would fit. And if you like the condo, do you like it because of the way it's furnished, or because it meets your needs? Because staged units feel more like a home, they pull on your emotional heart strings.

Take a step back and detach. Once you start buying on emotion, you will overpay.

16. Not Inspecting the Grounds and Common Area

Without even looking at a condominium's financial statements, I can have a good idea of how well the community is managed just by walking the property. Things like peeling paint, stains in the hallway carpet, or even visible rodent traps are signs that something might be amiss.

You do not need to check every corner of the common grounds for overgrown grass or visible dust, but do keep a keen eye on the condition of the community. Some older buildings might be in sparkling condition while some newer buildings could be showing their age much sooner than expected.

17. Not Having an Understanding of Who Lives in the Community

As a real estate agent, any conversations about demographics are off-limits or the real estate police will come after me. Since your real estate agent cannot discuss what type of person (age, race, skin color, etc.) lives in the condominium community because of Fair Housing laws, it will be up to you when you tour the building to make that determination.

Whether you are looking to age-in-place or you are right out of college with your first "real" job and are a fan of happy hours and "thirsty Thursdays," it will be important to you that you're living in a community that meshes with your lifestyle.

There's one building in my town of Arlington that has amazing units, but the second you walk into the lobby, it feels like you are walking into a retirement home. Every client that I have brought there under 40 years old says the same thing.

And on the flip side, there are some condos in my area that feel like a college dorm.

When you are touring a building, take note of who you see walking in and out of the elevator. Some communities have a bulletin board of activities. Take a look; is bridge an activity or is there a beer-tasting event?

One last note is to ask the concierge. If there is someone at the front desk, they see hundreds of residents each day and will be more likely to discuss what type of people live in the community.

18. Not Checking to See If the Community Is in a Flight Zone

Recently, I was in San Diego and my buddy who lives there brought us to the "hip" neighborhood of Little Italy. To give him credit, it was a pretty sweet neighborhood, but for those of you that know San Diego, the neighborhood is literally right next to the airport.

I felt like I was on that beach in St. Maarten where the planes fly right overhead. You seriously could not hear someone talking when a plane was landing. How could anyone live in that neighborhood?

When you are touring a building, you may only be in the community for as little as 10 minutes. However long you are there, take note if there is an airport nearby. If there is, how is the noise? What are the flight paths?

Ironically enough, I live in a condo that's in a flight path. For the most part the planes stay over the Potomac River that separates Washington D.C. and Virginia, but there is one flight that flies directly overhead every night at 6:56 p.m. That thing is loud!

If you are sensitive to noise, own pets that may not like planes, or simply want some peace and quiet, be sure you are cognizant of any neighboring airports or flight paths.

19. Not Seeing or Placing Value in the Amenities

Even if you hate the gym, or never go swimming, or will never step foot into the business center, amenities inside of condo communities have a tremendous amount of value.

Make it a point of emphasis when you are viewing a building to see everything the community has to offer. Even if it has no value to you, if you plan on renting out your condo in the future, or when it comes time to resell the property, the next resident may place significant value on the amenities.

You will be paying hundreds of dollars per month for your condo fees, so it will be worth your time to see what that money actually goes towards. And if the amenities are out-of-date, dirty, or in need of repair, that may also signal that the community is not run well or that a major project is around the corner.

20. Falling in Love With the First Property You See

Do you believe in love at first sight? When it comes to condos, I hope not.

Unless you are absolutely, 100% sure that the first condo you see is right for you, it's probably best to view a few others before pulling the trigger.

You want to get a grasp of what's out there before committing.

I've had buyers that have bought the first condo they walked into, and I have also worked with clients that have seen 100+ condos and I'm still waiting for them to buy (I wish I was kidding).

Depending on how much research you have done and your timeframe, the best option is probably not the first condo you take a look at. Oh, and if that condo does turn out to be the best and someone scoops it up before you can write your offer, forget about it.

Comparing available condos to properties that are no longer for sale is a losing battle and it will dampen your search. Have a short memory when it comes to properties that are no longer on the open market.

21. Not Testing Your Cell Phone Reception Inside the Unit

Depending on your cell phone network, there are some buildings in which you may get no signal or disrupted service. Even if you have a major network like I do, for whatever reason, there are just some buildings in which cell phone reception is an issue.

One client of mine even told me that he has to walk to his sunroom to make a call!

Not having service in your own home is unacceptable. When you tour condos, take a peek down at your phone and open up your favorite app to make sure it will load.

Making a phone call at every condo you visit to ensure you have service is probably overkill. But do double-check your cell phone in condos that you are seriously considering so you are not in for a rude awakening when you move in.

22. Not Seeing Where Packages Are Delivered

If you are anything like me, your front door is the recipient of a never-ending stream of packages. And I don't know about you, but I check the shipping status and delivery date approximately one second after I purchase, and approximately 3,048 times before the package finally arrives at my door.

It is for this reason that you need to understand where packages get delivered. Some communities have packages that are left outside the building. Other condos have a front desk where you can pick them up anytime from 9 a.m. - 5 p.m. And if you work normal business hours, you will have to make alternative arrangements to get your packages.

The best situations I have found are communities that either have a 24-hour front desk, a separate package room, staff that will walk them up to your floor and drop them at your door, or all of the above.

Occasionally, I will order something online that I don't just want sitting outside for a long period of time when it's delivered. Try to find out where packages go, especially if you are looking in a busy community or neighborhood with lots of foot traffic.

23. Not Checking Whether Induction Cookware is Necessary

In new construction communities and condos at the top end of the market, induction ranges are becoming more common.

When I was doing the walk-through for the first million-dollar condo I sold, my buyers and I were struggling to figure out how the range turned on. We almost gave up on it until we searched the range model type online and found out that the unit was an induction range that required the right cookware. The range only heats up when the cookware is touching the range top.

If you do a lot of cooking or spend a lot of time in the kitchen and you buy a condo with an induction range, you may have to buy an entire new set of cookware, which can be a costly undertaking. Induction ranges are rare, but give the range a quick glance next time you are out touring properties.

24. Not Checking Whether a Washer/Dryer Can Be Installed

Most buyers I work with have in their search criteria that a washer/dryer in-unit is required.

For those buyers that do not have this in their criteria, the question often comes up whether or not a washer/dryer can be installed in the unit.

Usually, for larger buildings, the answer will be "No".

I have personally seen in smaller buildings that you can bring the issue up to the board and have washer/dryers approved to be installed into condo communities that previously did not include a washer/dryer. If you do take this route, estimate the costs and then double your estimation, because installing a washer/dryer is not cheap and you will inevitably run into delays and unexpected costs.

25. Not Opening the Windows in the Winter

I don't know about you, but when the spring time rolls around, I like fresh air! I like the breeze. I like to hang out on the balcony of my condo.

If you are touring condos in the winter, step out onto the balcony or open up the windows in the master bedroom. What do you hear? What do you smell?

These days many condos have windows that do an excellent job of keeping out noise. But if you like spending time with the windows open, what sort of noise will you be up against? Is there a bar below you? Loading dock? Fire station? Dog-walking area?

Just like you would turn off all the lights in the condo to understand the natural light, open up a window or two the next time you view properties to understand the noise in the community that you are viewing.

26. Not Seeing Past Cosmetic Issues

I blame HGTV. Buyers want shiny condos with new paint, sparkling kitchens, and flawless bathrooms. And who can blame them? So do I!

But I also know a good deal when I see it. Buyers can sometimes overlook a property if there's just one blurry picture online or if the unit is in need of a paint job and some updating.

It's one thing to pass on a condo if you're not interested in "flipping that condo." But it's another issue if you find the exact unit you want on the top floor with the nice view but you pass on it because it has carpet instead of hardwood and the paint job is from the '80s.

When you come across an issue with a condo, ask yourself if it will take significant capital and time to fix, or if it's just a cosmetic issue that you can take care of with the help of a weekend, a few friends, and a few beers.

27. Not Checking the Floor Plan

Staged condos, and even vacant units, can play tricks on your eyes. In condominiums, every square foot is valuable, so you want to make sure you can squeeze all your furniture into your condo.

When you are ready to write an offer on a condo, be sure you have doubled-checked the floor plan to make sure the dimensions will fit your furniture.

Unfortunately, for whatever reason, many condos listed for sale do not include floor plans. Consider strapping yourself with a tape measure or a laser measuring tool so that you can quickly verify room dimensions.

28. Not Checking the Internet Provider

In my area, and maybe in your area as well, there are two main internet providers. Their names are irrelevant, but one company is loved and the other is despised. People do everything they can to avoid this one company. But when it comes to living in a condo building, you may not have a choice.

While some condo buildings have multiple options, there are many buildings in my market that have a contract with just one provider. This means that you are essentially stuck with whomever has contracted with the building. Your options go from choosing between company A, B, and C, to choosing internet or no internet.

The solution is rather easy as you can ask the management office who the cable/internet providers are for the building. Or when you are touring a unit, sometimes you will see the cable box, which will give you at least a partial answer.

For those of you that are more picky regarding your internet provider, be sure to inquire before so that you are not stuck with a provider that you do not like.

29. Not Viewing the Loading Dock Elevator

This was a late addition to the list, as it was not on my radar until I had a client recently send me a video of his brand new $5,000 couch that would not fit in the elevator. They tried every way to squeeze it into the elevator, but they just could not get it to fit.

Maybe the stairs could be an option?

Well, he lives on the 20th story, and because of the weight of the couch, that idea was eventually ruled out.

One of the downsides of living in a condo is that, unless you are only going a few floors up, everything has to fit in the elevator. If it doesn't fit, it doesn't get to go inside the condo. Or you have the workout of your life by dragging it up the stairs. For those oversized-couch-loving condo dwellers, a quick glance at the loading dock elevator can save you a big headache.

30. Not Learning What Percentage of Units Are Owner-Occupied

It can be difficult to understand the demographics and ambiance of a condominium community if you are not living in the community.

One way to understand more about the community is to find out the percentage of units that are owner-occupied, and the percentage that are renter-occupied.

Those communities with more renters are usually younger and louder. Communities with more owner-occupied residents are usually older and quieter.

It is easy to make blanket statements like the one above, and there's obviously exceptions to the rules, but for the most part, communities with more renters are a little bit different than a building with mostly owners.

If you are looking to downsize and lead a quieter life, maybe it is not wise to move into a community where every other unit is a renter.

Although, on the other hand, if you are only looking to live in your condo for a few years before turning your condo into an investment property, communities that have lots of renters show you that renters value the building and that there is a demand to rent in the community once you have moved out.

Section 3. Writing Your Offer and Going Under Contract (Opening Escrow)

31. Always Offering X% Below the List Price

A few summers ago, I was working with a first-time home buyer who was looking to purchase a one-bedroom condo with a balcony, hardwood floors, and a view. While seemingly simple to find, these condos are usually in high demand because those three aforementioned features are tougher to find than it sounds.

Eventually, when we would find a condo that met her criteria, she would consult with her brother (who was a real estate agent in another state), and we would offer 97.5% of the list price.

The three times we submitted offers, we were met with three multiple-offer scenarios, and as you may imagine, our offer lost three times in a row.

After the third time, my client confided in me that she was disappointed and did not know what we were doing wrong.

I was shocked. I was not shocked because our offers kept losing. I was shocked because she did not realize why we were losing. The whole time I was coaching her on how competitive the market is, the type of offer a seller is expecting the first weekend the property is listed, and how to beat out the other offers.

My advice had gone in one ear and out the other. There needs to be logic and reasoning behind the offers that you are submitting. In this scenario, 97.5% of the list price put us $10,000 below competing offers! We were not even close!

When you are coming up with the background on why you are submitting your offer at a certain point, you better have a better reason than "My brother who does real estate in South Carolina said I should do it this way."

All of this information was received, and none of it was implemented.

Looking back, it was my mistake for not sitting her down and isolating the strategy.

Where did the 97.5% price come from and why were we using that?

What experience does the brother have in purchasing real estate in the D.C. market?

Since we had lost out on two properties by using this strategy, how can we adjust our strategy to ensure that we are the best offer on the third property?

If and when you negotiate, there should be solid comparable properties or evidence to back up your numbers. If there are not solid comps or logical reasoning to why you are submitting your low offer, then you should not be disappointed when your desired outcome is not achieved.

If you take one thing from this tip, it is the following: do not take advice on negotiating from your brother/uncle/relative/college roommate/etc who is unfamiliar with your market.

32. Using the Wrong Comparable Properties (Comps) to Justify Price

When determining what price to offer on a condominium for sale, you will be researching previous condos that have sold in the community. The two biggest factors to focus on are recency and tier.

One of the best factors is recency, which will focus on condos that have sold in the past few months. This will give you the best idea of the value in the community. Have condos sold for more than list price? Were units sold in the first week they were on the market? Once you start going back a year, or even two years, the value and market may have been very different. The best comps will usually be the most recent.

As you are looking at the most recent units that have sold in the building, try to focus on those condos that are in the same "tier," i.e. if you're looking at buying #710, look at the "10" tier and see if #810, #910, #610, #510 have sold recently. The reason to do this is that other units in the tier will have the most in common with the property that is for sale. Things like square feet, view, and location within the building will all be a constant, making it much easier to determine value.

In many high-rise buildings, each level you go higher can equate to $3,000 and maybe even $10,000. And if you have a view of the river or D.C. monuments, that could be a $25,000 value or more! These factors are hard to attribute if you are just looking at the numbers on a piece of paper. So if you're trying to compare a second-level unit with a different view and layout to a 20th-floor unit, your numbers just won't add up. Focus on recency and tier, and then expand your comps as necessary from there.

33. Buying New Construction Without Negotiating

New construction condo communities will often have flexibility when it comes to the sales price and closing costs, and you may even be able to get a better rate on your mortgage if you use the building's preferred lender. If you do decide to use the preferred lender, be sure you call at least one other local lender in your area to confirm that the "deal" you are getting is in fact a good deal.

Depending on your market and the speed at which the condo community is selling, it's worth a shot to drive a hard bargain. At a recent new construction project in my area, one community was offering a $15,000 incentive for contracts that closed by a certain date.

Know your market and how competitive the new construction sales are in order to determine if a steep discount is possible in your market. Even in the competitive markets of Northern Virginia and D.C., if sales start falling behind, developers have an extra motivation to sell the last few condos and move on to their next project. This extra motivation could turn out to be a huge discount to you.

34. Not Doing a Radon Inspection If You Are on the Ground Level

For condos that are at or below grade, it is highly recommended that you conduct a radon inspection before settlement on the property.

Radon is a colorless, odorless gas that can cause cancer. The gas is present in soil at very low levels, and issues arise when the gas enters your condo and becomes trapped.

The chance of radon in a condo is rare because since the gas seeps in from the dirt, usually only basements and underground rooms would be affected. However, if you are on the ground level it may be worth it to conduct a radon inspection for your own good. The inspection costs anywhere from $99 - $199.

If high levels of radon are found, there are both short-term and long-term ways to remove the gas.

Contact your local radon or home inspection company for more information on radon tests and radon remediation.

35. Not Checking for Multiple Tax Records

As more purchasers are considering condos, and especially those that are moving from a house and are looking to downsize but are still in need of a large floor plan, combining condominium units is becoming more popular.

Depending on when the unit was converted, the owner (or previous owner) may have combined the two tax records, or there may still be two tax records out there. If you are planning on purchasing a condo that has been combined with another unit, be sure you are verifying the tax records before you write the offer.

Hypothetically, if you were to have your offer accepted but the contract only includes one tax record,, that would mean you are technically the owner of just part of the home.

Now, you may be thinking, "Matt, this is such a hypothetical situation, it would never happen in real life."

Well, I can tell you that my clients and I experienced it at first hand. There were two tax records, and only one was included in the contract. I missed the mistake, my clients missed it, the seller,

seller's agent, and even the title company all assumed there was just one tax record.

After about three months, the previous owner received a property tax bill from the unit that he technically still owned! My clients had paid for their condo but technically, the former owner still owned the third bedroom and dining room!

Correcting the mistake was an unpleasant experience for all parties that almost resulted in my clients suing the seller. Thankfully, before we got to this point, we came to a resolution and fixed things back to the way they should have been.

Let me make the mistakes for you... Double-check the tax record on the contract to the one in the property tax records to make sure you or your client is buying the correct property.

36. Not Checking Current Litigation

In its simplest form, condo associations are businesses. They are associations or corporations in charge of managing and overseeing a property or a community of properties. Occasionally, an individual owner may feel like they have been wronged somehow and will file suit against the condo association. While this may seem like an aggressive undertaking by the individual, it is a lot more common than you may believe.

Reasons that a condo board or association may get sued include common area maintenance upkeep failures, election disputes, an attempt by a resident to restrict board privileges, or even something as small as a pet dispute or a qualm over a parking spot.

Depending on the magnitude and timing of the litigation, an issue like this could cause a delay in acquiring financing for the purchase. If there is current litigation, your lender should be well-versed in the suit once they receive the condo questionnaire, so be sure you are working with a local lender who understands the market and can comprehend whether this will be a significant issue or not. Past litigation will often not be a cause for concern and may be difficult to find, so the focus will be on any current litigation. Work with your lender to understand how or if a current litigation will affect your purchase.

37. Not Confirming Potential Renovations Are Allowed Before Purchasing

Purchasing a condo with immediate plans to renovate the unit and open up the floor plan is a great idea. Not checking in with the condo management to see if the renovations are feasible is a bad idea.

I was recently working with a client who was looking to put in an offer on a two-bedroom condo with a galley kitchen with the intention of knocking down one of the kitchen walls to open up the space. The condo would look much better with the wall taken out, and the value of the unit would increase.

Right before we were planning on making the offer, I called the management who informed me that, because of the condominium's stacks and pipes that were in the wall, my client's renovation plans would not be possible.

Could you imagine if my client had purchased the condo and was then hit with the surprise that the renovation would not be possible? They would be furious! And probably very upset at me, their agent, for not checking.

Don't assume your agent will check in with condo management if you are planning a renovation after you close on your condo. Be proactive and tell your agent to reach out to condo management or do it yourself to make sure your grand plans are possible.

38. Not Correctly Pricing Renovation Costs

A common prerequisite that I see many of my buyers looking for is hardwood floors. Condos with carpet in the living room are often skipped over and not even considered, even if they come at a better price.

Well, what's stopping a buyer from going after a condo in need of some upgrades at a lower price and then putting in the upgrades they want?

Nothing.

Unfortunately, the HGTV-obsessed buyers in my market (and probably yours too) are too impressionable when it comes to units with shiny stainless steel appliances and sleek hardwood floors, even if the unit is priced at a premium.

Consider looking at condos that need a little work. You will have less competition when you put in an offer. And if you can factor in the correct renovation costs for installing hardwood floors or putting in a granite countertop or a new vanity, you can save yourself a lot of time and money instead of going after those picture-perfect units.

39. Not Seeing the Move-In Fee

Almost every condominium will have a move-in fee that the new owner or resident will have to pay. These fees can range from $100 to $700, with the majority falling between $200 and $400 depending on the community. When you purchase a condo, the move-in fee can be wrapped into the closing documents and paid for at settlement, but it is not always the case.

Paying for the move-in fee at settlement is usually preferred so you do not have to deal with cutting one extra check. If you are purchasing a condo as an investment to rent out or if your condo association that you are buying into only accepts move-in fees at the time of move-in, you will have to wait to pay this charge.

The situation to avoid is to either a) not know there is a move-in fee or b) think you already paid for this at closing. Cutting a $400 check to your new condo overlords is not a good "Welcome Home" gift. The condo docs or your real estate agent will be a good resource for the move-in fee amount. Be sure you know the move-in fee amount and when the fee will be paid as you move through the condo-buying process.

40. Not Knowing If There Is a Commercial Component of the Condominium Development

While some condominiums are stand-alone structures that only include the owner's residences, more and more urban developments are becoming mixed-use, where a condominium and hotel may share the same building or parts of the same property.

Mortgage lenders will not lend in condo communities that have a large commercial component. The most common occurrence you will come across is when a hotel and condominium share the same building. There are separate entrances, and usually the hotel will take up the first few floors, while the condominium residences will be located on the floors above the hotel. Because of the way these condo communities are laid out, you would never see hotel guests inside the building unless there is a shared common space, like a fitness center or something along those lines.

The commercial component percentage to watch out for starts at around 25% of the entire community. Obviously, there's no way to know the exact percentage just by looking at a community, which is why it is vital that you are working with a real estate agent who understands the nuances of each building.

You should be OK if there is ground-floor retail, but once you start seeing multiple floors of retail, an office building, or a hotel in the same building or space as the condo association, you may have to get special financing to move forward on the property. The building management should have a list of approved lenders in the community that they can provide.

41. Thinking All-Cash Will Result in a Large Discount

Purchasing with all-cash is the best type of financing in the eyes of the seller because there is very little worry that the buyer will fail to perform. Compared to an FHA loan or VA loan, which might cause headaches and delays, using all-cash is definitely more sought-after and preferred.

But how much better is all-cash than, say, a 20% down conventional loan?

If there are multiple offers on a property, the seller will consider every single aspect of each contract. The sales price will be at the top of the list for sellers.

When it comes to multiple offers, there is a growing trend among buyers that using all-cash with a lower sales price is better than a financed offer at a higher sales price.

This is simply not true.

To the seller, money is money. It doesn't matter if it's coming via cash or a mortgage. As long as the competing offer that is using a mortgage has strong terms and extremely well-qualified purchasers, using all-cash will not warrant a significant discount.

If you do plan on using all-cash for your purchase and are preparing for a multiple-offer situation, be sure to ask the seller (or have your agent ask the seller's agent) when their preferred closing date would be.

Time is money. Even if another financed offer comes in higher than yours, it will still take that mortgage at least 21 days to close. Depending on the seller's preference on settlement date, you as an all-cash buyer can close literally the next week if it works for the seller and makes sense for the deal.

42. Not Checking for Special Assessments

When purchasing a condominium, there are many things that you will be able to control. A potential special assessment levied upon the owners of a condominium community will not be one of those things.

The best way to go about seeing if there is an upcoming special assessment will be to read through the condo documents. The downside is that you usually will be receiving the condo docs *after* your offer is accepted. You can also have your agent contact the listing agent before you submit the offer, and they will be able to tell you if there is an upcoming special assessment.

The Meeting Minutes section of the condo docs should shed light on any imminent assessments. Do not place too much emphasis into any third-party studies that recommend assessments in the distant future or things of that nature, as those studies and projects can change and are not concrete. What you want to focus on is actual conversation currently happening regarding any assessments.

43. Not Thoroughly Reading the Closing Disclosure

The Closing Disclosure (CD) provided at settlement outlines all the itemized costs associated with purchasing the home. Now, with whatever type of property you are buying, you will review through the CD. However, with condos, you will pay more attention because there are items on the CD that could have been paid already or could be paid by you in the future, outside of the CD.

The two biggest items are the condo move-in fee and the condo dues for the month following the month that you settle in. Many associations allow you to pay for the move-in fee at settlement and then the title company simply wires the funds to the condo association. But what if you're purchasing the property as an investment unit? Or what if you want to pay the fee to the association directly?

Unless you say otherwise, the title company will include the condo move-in fee in the CD. If you've already made arrangements outside of settlement to take care of this, be sure you have notified the title company.

The same goes for the condo fee. While the current month's condo fee will be due at settlement and pro-rated if necessary, the condo fee for next month is usually also included. If you would rather pay next month's condo fee directly to the condo association rather than at closing, notify your title company of the changes so there aren't extra fees on your CD at settlement.

Section 4. Living in the Condo

44. Not Understanding When You Can Move In

Holidays, weekends, and even after 5 p.m. may be times that are off-limits for moving into your new community. Depending on the condominium, there will be move-in policies that you will have to follow, and some may be a little more strict than what you might expect.

I was talking with a resident in my condo building who said that he had to stop his move because the clock had struck 5 p.m. and every 15 minutes after 5 p.m., he was told he would have been fined by the condo management.

This is obviously on the more extreme scale for move-ins, but it's worth pointing out.

Be sure you fully understand the move-in policy, fees, time frame allowed, and give yourself enough time, both in alerting the management staff and when it comes to your move so you do not run out of time like my neighbor.

45. Assuming You Have No Rules to Follow in Your Condo

Just because you own property and everything "inside the walls" is yours, that unfortunately does not mean you have free reign to impose whatever lifestyle habits you choose. There are still some restrictions, and I will touch on two of the biggest hindrances for condo owners.

The first rule that most condo buyers seem to forget is with regards to covering hardwood floors. Most condos in my area stipulate that 80% of hardwood floors must be covered by an area rug to help with noise abatement. This is especially vital for older communities that have undergone renovations from carpet to hardwood floors. Noise travelling to the unit below is a major concern for condo owners and renters alike. While the likelihood is rare, if your downstairs neighbor complains to management, you may have to add a rug to comply with the rules or you could face a fine.

The second major rule I see owners breaking all the time is with regards to balconies. In the bylaws of the condo documents, there is usually an explanation about what can and cannot be stored on balconies. Large bulky items like bikes, storage boxes, gas grills, and other items are often forbidden on balconies.

The most egregious example I have seen of a condo resident breaking this rule was a few years ago, when I helped a landlord find a tenant for her condo. That new tenant was international and was not as well-versed with the customs and rules here in the States. Halfway into her lease, I was cc'd on an email to her from the condo management office stating that she had to remove her raw chicken hanging off the balcony. This tenant was hang-drying her dinner from her balcony, which is within feet of a handful of other people's homes! Even though I probably have not read the condo documents for the community you are interested in, I will go out on a limb here and say that hanging raw food from the balcony is not permitted in your association either.

46. Not Thinking About Resale Value

When looking at condos to purchase, spend a minute to think long-term about what's wrong with the condo and how the unit may be difficult to sell in the future.

One example of this would be a large two-bedroom two-bath unit (1,300 square feet) in my building that installed a pocket door in the wall that separates the bedroom. The condo is now essentially a 1 BR + den or even just a 1 BR with a very large master suite. Oh yeah, and it's priced almost at $700,000!

That price would be in the ballpark for a two-bed two-bath unit, but since the owners made a significant renovation, they have hurt their chances at capturing a large part of the two-bedroom buyer market.

Sure, it could be easy to fix the door back into a wall, but that takes time and effort, and most buyers will not want to pay for the extra work to be done, especially if a unit is already priced at the top of the market.

Whether you are searching for a condo to buy or are living in a condo and thinking about some upgrades, think long-term about how these changes may affect the property's value when you go to sell (or rent) the condo in the future.

———————————

Share the Knowledge

Thank you so much for reading this book. I hope you were able to take away valuable information that you can use in your upcoming home purchase.

If you found this book helpful and you think others would benefit from it, please leave a positive review on Amazon!

Referrals

If you, or anyone you know, is looking to purchase or sell a home in the Northern Virginia/D.C. area, please send me an email at matt@orangelinecondo.com.

If you are looking for a real estate agent in your city to help you with your real estate purchase, I have a network of top-producing agents that are located all across the country. Send me an email with where you are looking to purchase and a few details about your search, and I would be honored to put you in touch with one of my top-producing agents.

Contact Information

I would love to connect with you! You can find me here:

Email: matt@OrangeLineCondo.com
YouTube: YouTube.com/TheMattLeighton
Facebook: Facebook.com/TheMattLeighton
Twitter: Twitter.com/TheMattLeighton
LinkedIn: Linkedin.com/in/themattleighton/

Brokerage details:
Century 21 Redwood Realty
1934 Wilson Blvd
Arlington, VA 22201
703-790-1850

42449612R00027

Made in the USA
Middletown, DE
14 April 2019